# FIRST UNITED METHODIST CHURCH

# GAINESVILLE, GEORGIA

# NARTHEX AND SANCTUARY

# STAINED GLASS WINDOWS

# COLORING BOOK

IN MEMORY OF

REVEREND JIM THOMPSON

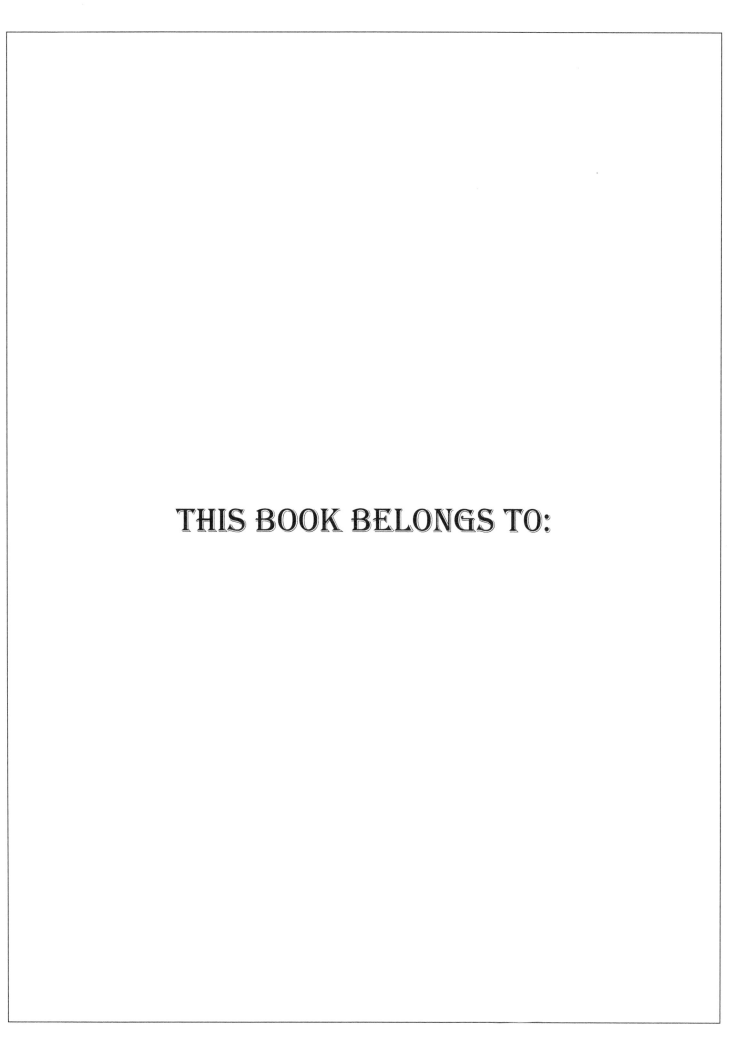

THIS BOOK BELONGS TO:

THE NARTHEX

VIEWED FROM INSIDE

THE ONGOING CHURCH

TOP CENTER WINDOW

*PENTECOST*

TOP LEFT WINDOW

*PAUL'S CONVERSION*

TOP RIGHT WINDOW

*PETER'S ROOFTOP VISION*

# PENTECOST

## Acts 2:1-4

*Now when the day of Pentecost had come, they were all together in one place. Suddenly a sound like a violent wind blowing came from heaven and filled the entire house where they were sitting. And tongues spreading out like a fire appeared to them and came to rest on each one of them. All of them were filled with the Holy Spirit, and they began to speak in other languages as the Spirit enabled them.*

# PAUL'S CONVERSION

## Acts 9:1-7

*Meanwhile, Saul was still breathing out murderous threats against the Lord's disciples. He went to the high priest and asked him for letters to the synagogues in Damascus, so that if he found any there who belonged to the Way, whether men or women, he might take them as prisoners to Jerusalem. As he neared Damascus on his journey, suddenly a light from heaven flashed around him. He fell to the ground and heard a voice say to him, "Saul, Saul, why do you persecute me?"*

*"Who are you, Lord?" Saul asked.*

*"I am Jesus, whom you are persecuting," he replied. "Now get up and go into the city, and you will be told what you must do."*

# PETER'S ROOFTOP VISION

### Acts 10:9-13

*About noon the following day as they were on their journey and approaching the city, Peter went up on the roof to pray. He became hungry and wanted something to eat, and while the meal was being prepared, he fell into a trance. He saw heaven opened and something like a large sheet being let down to earth by its four corners. It contained all kinds of four-footed animals, as well as reptiles and birds. Then a voice told him, "Get up, Peter. Kill and eat."*

THE NARTHEX

EARLY INFLUENTIAL THEOLOGINS

LEFT PANEL

TOP TO BOTTOM

*SEAL OF ST. AUGUSTINE OF HIPPO*

*SEAL OF MARTIN LUTHER*

*SEAL OF JOHN CALVIN*

# St. Augustine of Hippo

After Paul one of the most widely read and influencial theologins of all time.

354-430 A.D.

## His Seal

# A Flaming Heart Transfixed by Two Arrows

# MARTIN LUTHER

Father of the Great Reformation.

1483-1546 A.D.

## HIS SEAL

# A Black Cross Within a Red Heart on a White Rose

# JOHN CALVIN

Successor to Martin Luther as the preeminent Protestant theologin.

1509-1564 A.D.

## HIS SEAL

# An Outstreached Hand with a Heart

# THE NARTHEX

## EARLY METHODISM

### RIGHT SIDE PANEL

### TOP TO BOTTOM

*JOHN WESLEY'S COAT OF ARMS*

*CHARLES WESLEY'S SYMBOLS OF MUSIC*

*FRANCIS ASBURY ON A HORSE IN FRONT OF A BIBLE*

## JOHN WESLEY

The Father of Methodism.

1703-1791 A.D.

## HIS COAT OF ARMS

## A Cross with Five Shells

# CHARLES WESLEY

1707-1708 A.D.

## MUSIC SYMBOLS

## The Word "HARK"

Charles Wesley was the author of many of our Methodist hymns. The one most famous was "Hark the Herald Angles Sing" which this symbol acknowledges.

There are 65 of Charles Wesley's songs in the United Methodist Hymnal.

## The Treble Clef

# FRANCIS ASBURY

Francis Asbury was a circuit rider and the General Superintendent of the Methodist Societies in the United States of America in the late 1700s and early 1800s. He was responsible for the dramatic growth of Methodism during that time.

1745-1816 A.D

## Asbury on a Horse in Front of a Bible

THE SANCTUARY

OLD TESTATMENT SIDE/COURTYARD

LEFT LANCET

THE PATRIARCHS

*THE HAND OF GOD*

*THE RAM IN THE BUSH*

*MOSES*

*THE PASSOVER*

*JOSHUA AND HIS TRUMPET*

# THE HAND OF GOD

Genesis 1:26

*Then God said, "Let Us make man in Our image, according to Our likeness; let them have dominion over the fish of the sea, over the birds of the air, and over the cattle, over all the earth and over every creeping thing that creeps on the earth."*

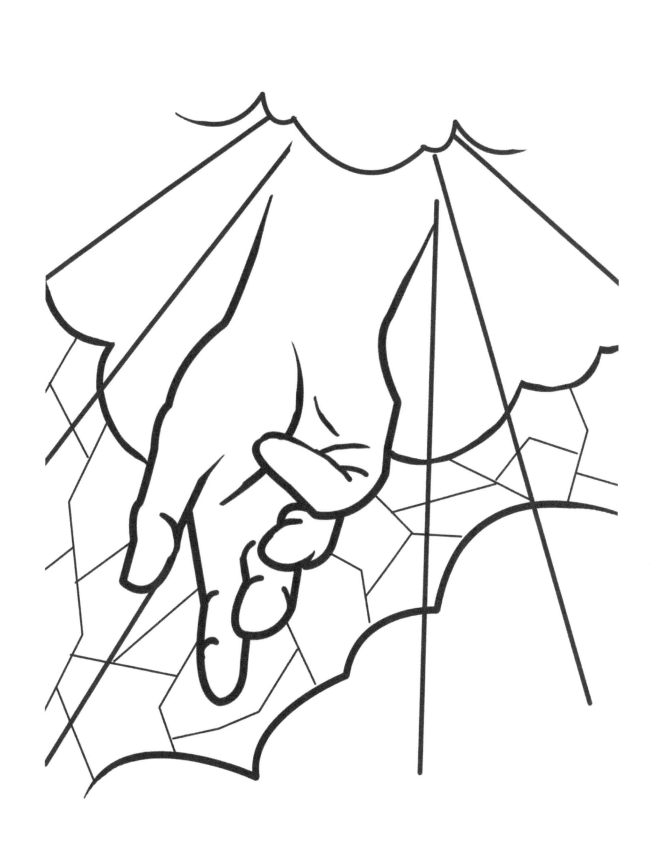

# RAM IN THE BUSH

Genesis 22:11-14

*And Abraham lifted up his eyes, and looked, and behold behind him a ram caught in a thicket by his horns: and Abraham went and took the ram, and offered him up for a burnt offering in the stead of his son.*

# MOSES AND THE TEN COMMANDMENTS

Exodus 24:12

*The LORD said to Moses, "Come up to me on the mountain and stay here, and I will give you the tablets of stone with the law and commandments I have written for their instruction."*

# PASSOVER

Exodus 12:12-13

*On that same night I will pass through Egypt and strike down every firstborn of both people and animals, and I will bring judgment on all the gods of Egypt. I am the Lord. The blood will be a sign for you on the houses where you are, and when I see the blood, I will pass over you. No destructive plague will touch you when I strike Egypt.*

# JOSHUA AND HIS TRUMPET

Joshua 6:20

*So the people shouted when the priests blew with the trumpets: and it came to pass,*

*when the people heard the sound of the trumpet, and the people shouted with a great*

*shout, that the wall fell down flat, so that the people went up into the city, every man*

*straight before him, and they took the city.*

# OLD TESTAMENT SIDE/COURTYARD

## CENTER LANCET

### THE PROPHETS

*JESUS*

*THE LOCUST/AMOS*

*ISAIAH*

*THE RAINBOW COVENANT*

*DANIEL AND THE LIONS*

*JONAH AND THE WHALE*

# JESUS THE PROPHET

Mathew 21:11

*And the multitude said this is Jesus the prophet of Nazareth of Galilee.*

# THE LOCUST

Amos 7:1-3

*Thus the Lord G*OD *showed me: Behold, He formed locust swarms at the beginning of the late crop; indeed it was the late crop after the king's mowings. And so it was, when they had finished eating the grass of the land, that I said:"O Lord G*OD*, forgive, I pray!*

*Oh, that Jacob may stand, For he is small!"*

*So the L*ORD *relented concerning this. "It shall not be," said the L*ORD*.*

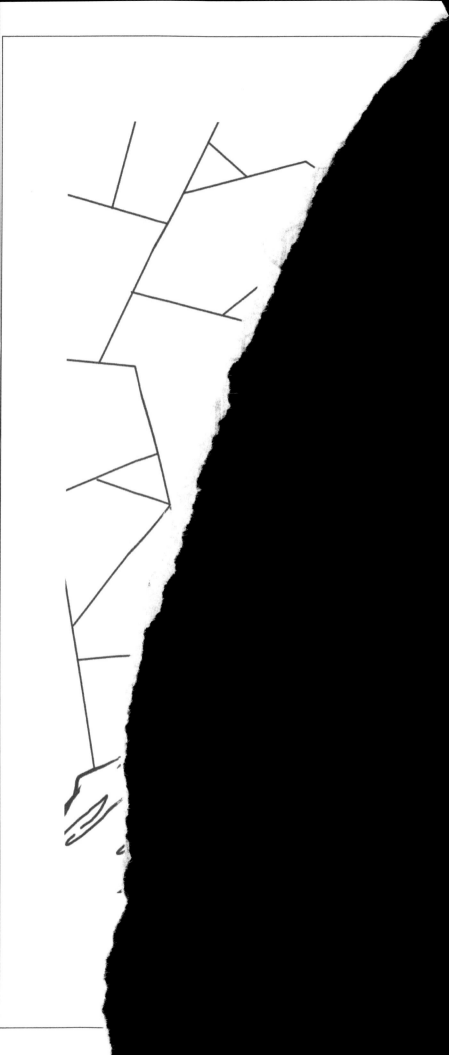

*s; upon him*

*healed.*

# THE RAINBOW COVENANT

## Genesis 9:15-17

*And I will remember my covenant, which is between me and you and every living creature of all flesh; and the waters shall no more become a flood to destroy all flesh. And the bow shall be in the cloud; and I will look on it, that I may remember the everlasting covenant between God and every living creature of all flesh that is on the earth. And God said to Noah, This is the token of the covenant, which I have established between me and all the flesh that is on earth.*

# DANIEL AND THE LIONS

Daniel 6:22

*"My God sent his angel and he shut the mouths of the lions. They have not hurt me, because I was found innocent in his sight. Nor have I ever done any wrong before you, O king."*

# JONAH AND THE WHALE

Jonah 1:17

*Now the LORD had prepared a great fish to swallow up Jonah. And Jonah was in the belly of the fish three days and three nights.*

# OLD TESTAMENT SIDE/COURTYARD

## RIGHT LANCET

## THE KINGS

### THE COMPLETED TEMPLE

### DAVID AND HIS HARP

### SOLOMON AND THE SCALES OF JUSTICE

# THE COMPLETED TEMPLE

1 Chronicles 22:19

*Now devote your heart and soul to seeking the LORD your God. Begin to build the sanctuary of the LORD God, so that you may bring the ark of the covenant of the LORD and the sacred articles belonging to God into the temple that will be built for the Name of the LORD.*

# KING SOLOMON

1 kings 3:25-27

*The king said, "Divide the living child in two, and give half to the one and half to the other." Then the woman whose child was the living one spoke to the king, for she was deeply stirred over her son and said, "Oh, my lord, give her the living child, and by no means kill him." But the other said, "He shall be neither mine nor yours; divide him!" Then the king said, "Give the first woman the living child, and by no means kill him. She is his mother."*

# DAVID AND HIS HARP

1 Samuel 16:23

*And whenever the tormenting spirit from God troubled Saul, David would play the harp.*

*Then Saul would feel better, and the tormenting spirit would go away.*

# NEW TESTAMENT SIDE/LAKE

## LEFT LANCET

## EARLY MINISTRY OF JESUS

*THE BABY JESUS AND THE MANGER*

*JESUS CALLING THE DISCIPLES*

*THE DOVE AND WATER FROM A SHELL*

*(SYMBOLS OF BAPTISM AND THE HOLY SPIRIT)*

# BABY JESUS IN THE MANGER

Luke 2:7

*And she brought forth her firstborn Son, and wrapped Him in swaddling cloths, and laid*

*Him in a manger, because there was no room for them in the inn.*

# JESUS CALLING THE DISCIPLES

Mathew 4:18-20

*As Jesus was walking beside the Sea of Galilee, he saw two brothers, Simon called Peter and his brother Andrew. They were casting a net into the lake, for they were fishermen. "Come, follow me," Jesus said, "and I will send you out to fish for people." At once they left their nets and followed him.*

# WATER AND THE DOVE-BAPTISM AND THE HOLY SPIRIT

Mathew 3:16

*As soon as Jesus was baptized, he went up out of the water. At that moment heaven was*

*opened, and he saw the Spirit of God descending like a dove and alighting on him.*

NEW TESTAMENT SIDE/LAKE

CENTER LANCET

LIFE OF JESUS ON EARTH

*JESUS ASCENDED TO HEAVEN*

*THE SYMBOLS OF THE CROSS*

*THE PHOENIX*

*THE LAST SUPPER*

## JESUS ASCENDED TO HEAVEN AND CROWNED AS KING

Mark 16:19

*So then after the Lord had spoken unto them, he was received up into heaven, and sat*

*on the right hand of God.*

# THE CROSS AND SYMBOLS OF THE CRUCIFIXION

Mark 15:20

*And when they had mocked him, they took off the purple robe and put his own clothes on him. Then they led him out to crucify him.*

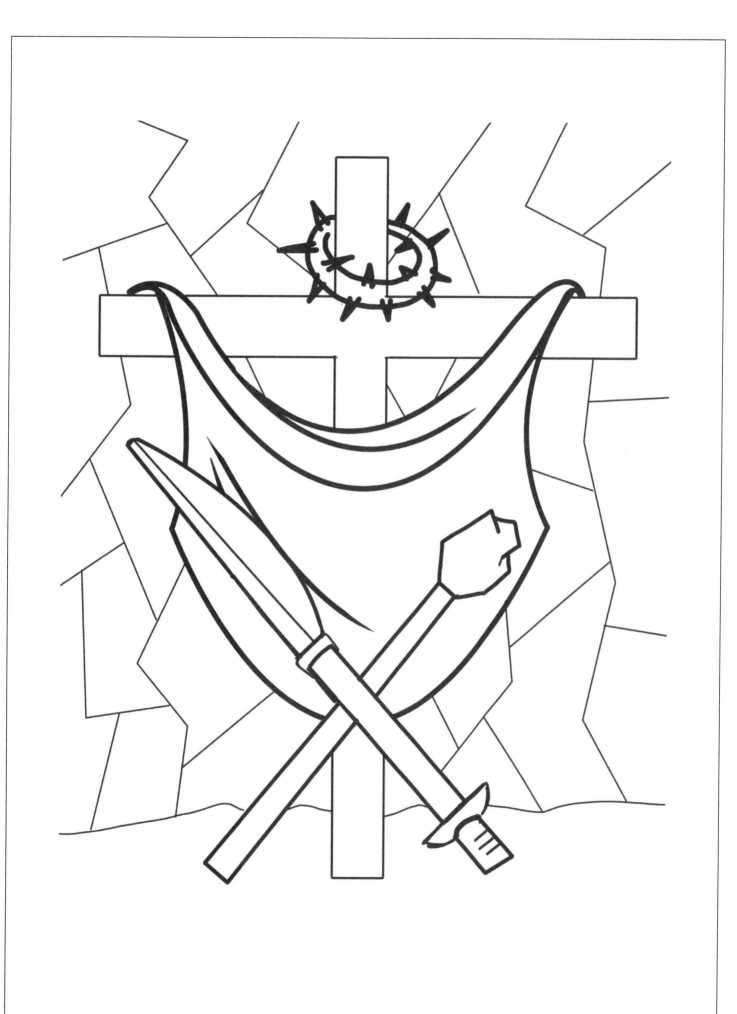

# THE PHOENIX SYMBOL OF THE RESURRECTION OF JESUS

*The mythical Phoenix is said to have built a nest, set it on fire and then to have risen from the ashes in victory. The Phoenix has become symbolic of the resurrection, immortality and the life-after-death of Jesus.*

# THE LAST SUPPER

### Luke 22:14-22

*When the hour came, Jesus and his apostles reclined at the table. And he said to them, "I have eagerly desired to eat this Passover with you before I suffer. For I tell you, I will not eat it again until it finds fulfillment in the kingdom of God." After taking the cup, he gave thanks and said, "Take this and divide it among you. For I tell you I will not drink again of the fruit of the vine until the kingdom of God comes." And he took bread, gave thanks and broke it, and gave it to them, saying, "This is my body given for you; do this in remembrance of me." In the same way, after the supper he took the cup, saying, "This cup is the new covenant in my blood, which is poured out for you."*

NEW TESTAMENT SIDE/LAKE

RIGHT LANCET

THE MIRACLES

THE LAMB AND THE ROD AND STAFF

THE MIRACLE AT CANA

THE HEALING OF THE BLEEDING WOMAN

JESUS PREACHING FROM A BOAT

John 10:11

*I am the good shepherd. The good shepherd lays down his life for the sheep.*

# THE WEDDING AT CANA-WATER TO WINE MIRACLE

John 2:1-4

*And the third day there was a marriage in Cana of Galilee; and the mother of Jesus was there. And both Jesus was called, and his disciples, to the marriage. And when they wanted wine, the mother of Jesus saith unto him, They have no wine. Jesus saith unto her, Woman, what have I to do with thee? Mine hour is not yet come.*

# THE BLEEDING WOMAN OF FAITH

Mark 5:24-29

*And a certain woman, which had an issue of blood twelve years, and had suffered many things of many physicians, and had spent all that she had, and was nothing bettered, but rather grew worse. When she had heard of Jesus, came in the press behind, and touched his garment. For she said, if I may touch but his clothes, I shall be whole. And straightway the fountain of her blood was dried up; and she felt in her body that she was healed of that plague.*

# JESUS PREACHING FROM THE BOAT

Mark 3:5-9

*Jesus withdrew with his disciples to the lake, and a large crowd from Galilee followed.*

*When they heard about all he was doing, many people came to him from Judea,*

*Jerusalem, Idumea, and the regions across the Jordan and around Tyre and Sidon.*

*Because of the crowd he told his disciples to have a small boat ready for him, to keep the*

*people from crowding him.*

*Where did the stained glass studio leave their mark?*

*Narthex Entrance/Right panel/Below Francis Asbury*

*(Man on a horse)*

December 2013

Jennie Cooper Press

660 A Lanier Park Dr.

Suite A

Gainesville, Ga.

Created by

John McHugh

Photography

John McHugh

Illustrations

Taryn Dufault

Karen McHugh